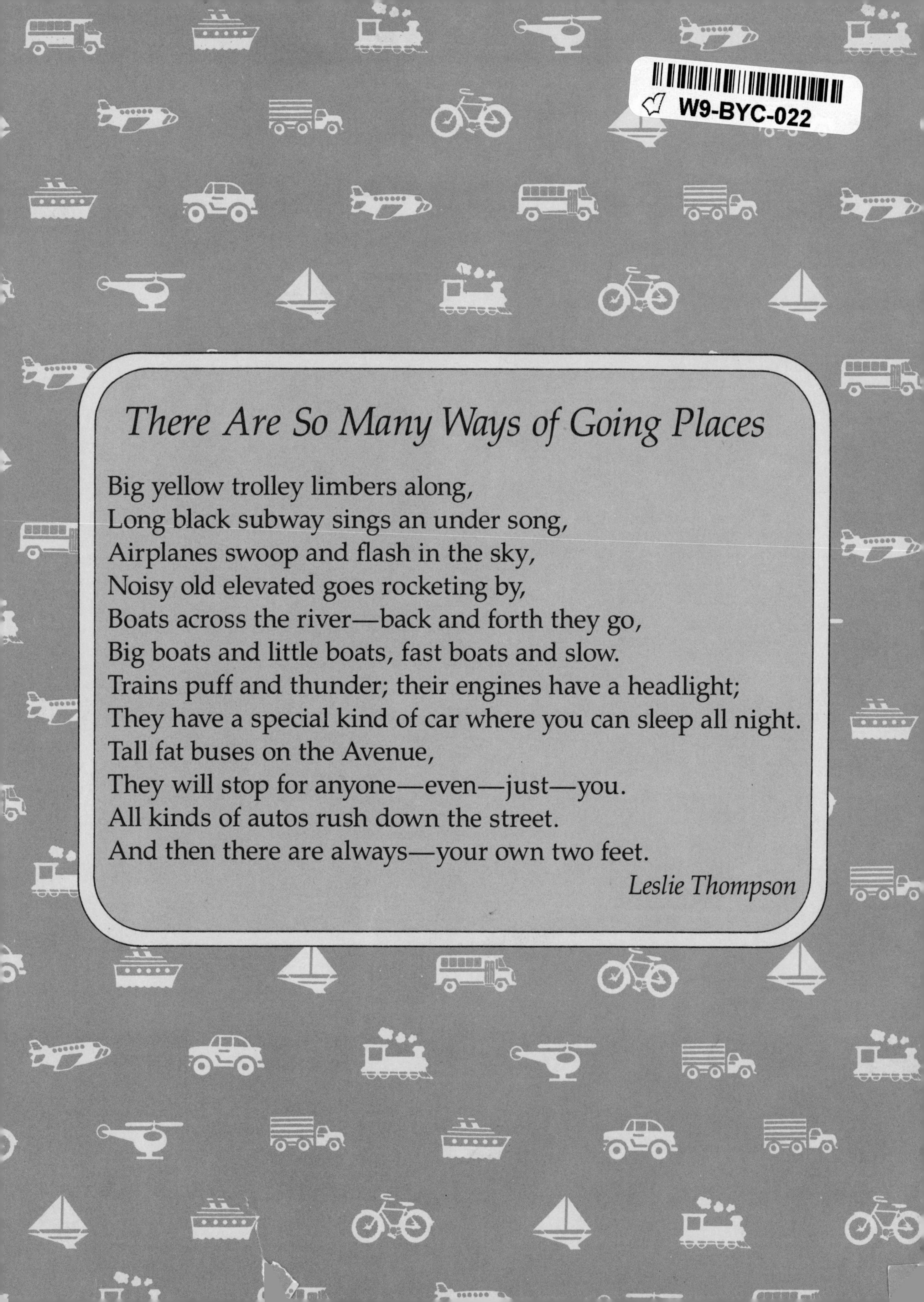

There Are So Many Ways of Going Places

Big yellow trolley limbers along,
Long black subway sings an under song,
Airplanes swoop and flash in the sky,
Noisy old elevated goes rocketing by,
Boats across the river—back and forth they go,
Big boats and little boats, fast boats and slow.
Trains puff and thunder; their engines have a headlight;
They have a special kind of car where you can sleep all night.
Tall fat buses on the Avenue,
They will stop for anyone—even—just—you.
All kinds of autos rush down the street.
And then there are always—your own two feet.

Leslie Thompson

Little People™ Big Book

About THINGS WE RIDE

ALEXANDRIA, VIRGINIA

Table of Contents

When We Play

When We Travel

When We Work

When We Play

Preferred Vehicles

A bicycle's fine for a little trip
Up the street or down:
An automobile for a longer trip,
Off to another town;
An airplane's fine for around the world,
To many a far-put place;
And a rocket, oh, for the longest trip
Away into outer space.

Leland B. Jacobs

COME RIDE WITH ME

Vroom and zoom
Come ride with me!
How many fun things to ride do you see?

Who's on the roller skates, racing through town?
Who's on the pogo stick, bouncing up and down?
Who's on the giant stilts, high in the air?
Who's on the scooter, scooting off somewhere?
Who's in the big balloon, drifting with the breeze?
Who's flying down the hill on a pair of skis?
Who's on the saucer? Who's on the sled?
Who's in the wagon, eating jam and bread?
Who's on the skateboard? Who's on the bike?
Who's in the inner tube? Who's on the trike?
Who's on the ice skates, twirling round and round?
Who's in the go-cart, speeding 'cross the ground?

Every time you look at this,
you might see something new.
I'd love to jump inside this page
and play there . . . wouldn't you?

Riding on My Bike

Riding on my bike –
That is what I like!
Like the wind
So fast I go,
Past the houses
In a row.
Now fast and faster,
Set the brake!
Down hill I go,
What speed I make!
Then up the hill
Without a stop,
I push and pedal
To the top,
I pedal hard,
I pedal fast:
Back home again
I come at last.

Lois Lenski

Types of Cycles

A *uni*cycle has 1 wheel – and no handlebars!
Uni means *one*.

A *bi*cycle has 2 wheels – both the same size, for a good steady ride.
Bi means *two*.

A *tri*cycle has 3 wheels – one big and two small.
Tri means *three*.

A *tandem* bicycle is a bicycle built for two.
It's like two bikes in one!

HISTORY OF THE BICYCLE

The first bicycle was made 200 years ago. Some of the first bicycles had no seats, no pedals, and no handlebars! They were just two wheels connected by a piece of wood. The rider climbed on and pushed with his feet to make them go. But people who loved bicycles kept thinking up new ways to make them better. Someone added handlebars. Someone else thought up a way to make pedals. After many years, and lots of new ideas, bicycles began to look like the bike you ride today.

This bicycle was called the Steerable Hobbyhorse. It had handlebars and a seat, but no pedals. The rider pushed it with his feet. The front of the seat curved upward so the rider could rest his chest on it while he pushed.

1820

The Macmillan bicycle was the first to have pedals. The pedals in the front turned the back wheel like a crank. It looks funny, but it worked pretty well!

1840

This was called the Safety Bicycle. You can see how alike it is to the ones used today!

This bicycle was called the Ariel. Its pedals turned the front wheel. The front wheel was so big it almost looked like a unicycle! Do you think you could ride one of these?

The Magic Red Sled

by Michael J. Pellowski

One snowy, winter day Benji Bunny's Uncle Al came to visit. Uncle Al was Benji's favorite uncle. He was a special rabbit. Al was short for Alakazam. Uncle Alakazam was a magician's rabbit. Whenever he came to visit his nephew Benji, he always brought the little bunny a magical present.

Once Uncle Al brought Benji a magical two-wheeled bike. The bike had invisible training wheels on it. Thanks to Uncle Al, Benji learned how to ride a two-wheeler.

Another time, Uncle Al gave Benji a magical wagon. The wagon didn't need to be pushed or pulled. Whenever Benji sat in it, the wagon rolled all by itself.

"This time I brought you something really special," Uncle Alakazam said to Benji.

"Oh, boy!" yelled Benji when he saw Uncle Al's latest gift. "A sleek red sled! Thank you, Uncle Al! I love sledding more than anything!" Benji cried. And he gave his Uncle Al a great big bunny hug.

"I know how much you like sledding," Uncle Al replied. "That is why I gave you this sled."

Benji smiled from ear to ear. He was sure the sleek red sled was magic. "Can I go outside and try my new sled?" he asked his mom and dad.

"Of course," Mrs. Bunny said. "Just dress warmly. It's very cold out in the snow."

"I know," shivered Benji. "Cold weather is the one part of sledding I don't like." Uncle Al chuckled as Benji walked away.

Benji dressed in his snowsuit. Then he took his sled and went outside. He pulled the sleek red sled up his favorite sledding hill. "I wonder what this magic sled can do?" Benji asked himself. "Will it go super fast? Will it steer itself around trees? What will it do?"

Benji Bunny hopped on his new sled. "Here I go!" he shouted. Zoom! The sled sped down the hill. It went fast. But it was not fast enough to be magic. Whoosh! Benji steered around trees and stumps. The sled did not steer itself. Slosh! The sled skidded to a stop.

"This sled is very nice," Benji said as he walked back up the hill. "I like it a lot. But it is not magic."

Zoom! Whoosh! Slosh! Zoom! Whoosh! Slosh! Up and down went Benji and his sled. Soon he was too cold to ride the sled anymore. Shivering from the tip of his floppy ears to the bottom of his fluffy tail, Benji went back inside.

"How did the sled work?" asked Uncle Al, smiling broadly.

"It worked great," said Benji. "A present doesn't have to be magic for me to like it," thought the little bunny. "That red sled is really something special," Benji said to his Uncle Al.

"It sure is," Uncle Alakazam admitted. He chuckled and walked away.

All winter, Benji had fun with his new red sled. Every time it snowed, he went sledding. Of course, Benji never stayed out too long in the cold because he didn't like the chilly weather.

Before long, spring came. The weather turned warm. Benji had fun in the warm sun. He skipped through fields of flowers. He swung on tree branches. And he rolled down his favorite sledding hill, which was now covered with grass.

One hot summer day, Benji couldn't think of anything new to do. It was too hot for skipping, swinging, or rolling. "Today would be a good day to go sledding," Benji said. "But a sled can't go without snow." Benji thought for a moment. "If I can't really go sledding, I'll pretend to ride," he decided.

Benji took his red sled out of the storage shed. He carried it up his favorite hill. The little bunny put the sled down on the grass. Onto the sled he hopped.

Zippity-zoom! Whoosh! Down the grassy hill sped the sleek red sled.

"WHEEE!" cried Benji in glee. "Uncle Al played a trick on me. "This sled really is magic. It doesn't need snow to slide on. Hooray for Uncle Al!"

Up and down the grassy hill went the happy little bunny on his magic red sled. And not once did he ever get the slightest bit cold.

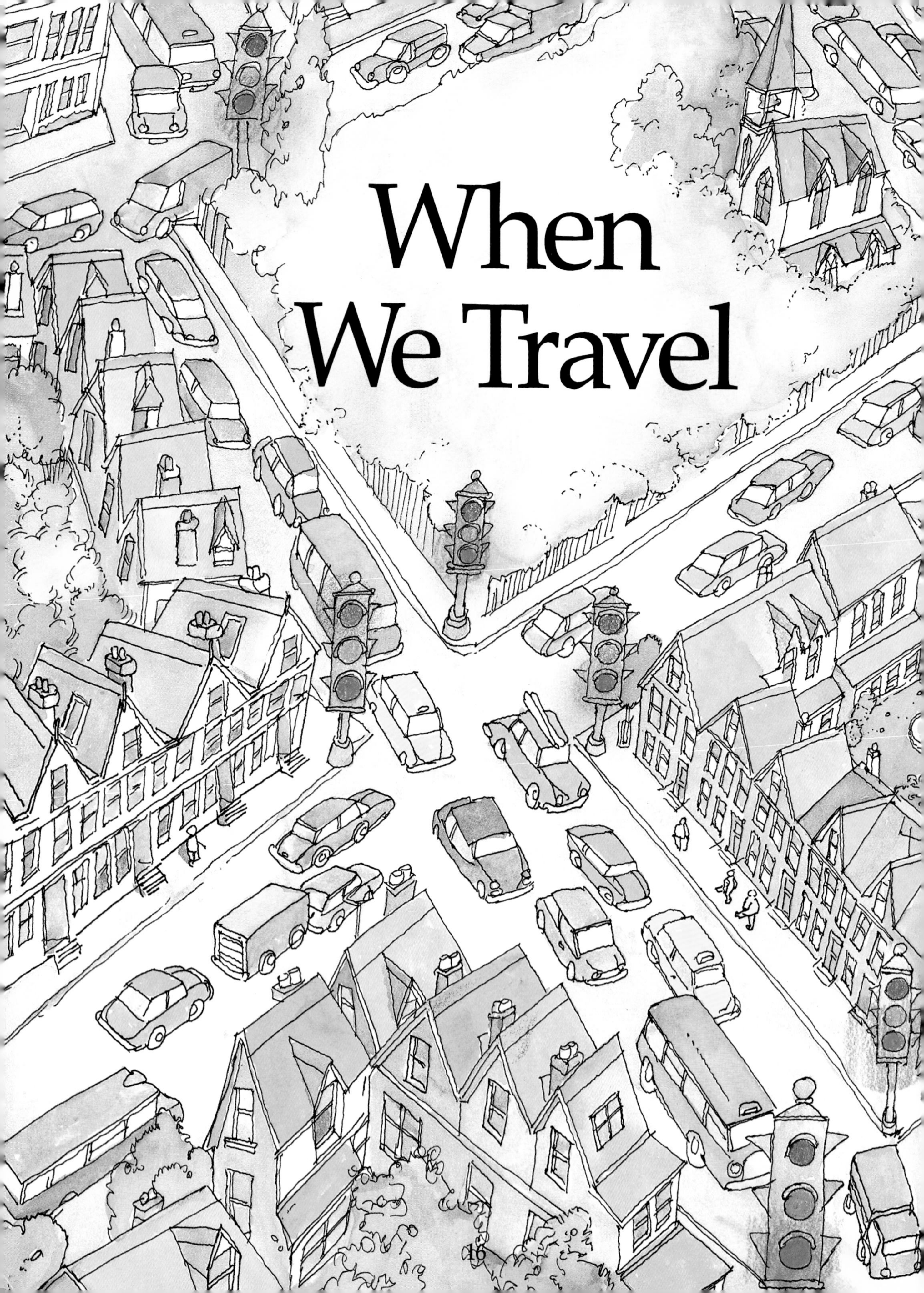

When We Travel

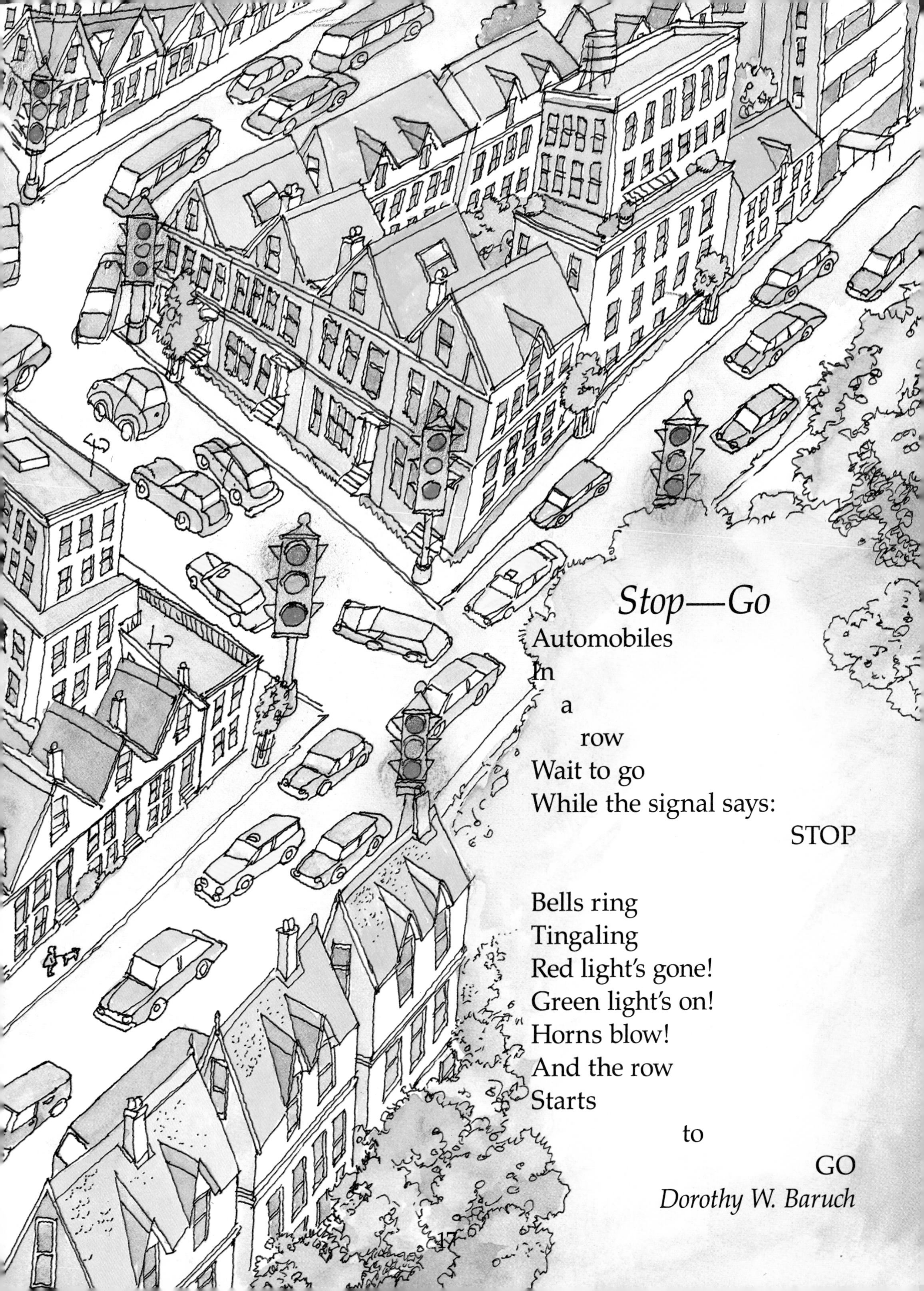

Stop—Go

Automobiles
In
  a
    row
Wait to go
While the signal says:
                                        STOP

Bells ring
Tingaling
Red light's gone!
Green light's on!
Horns blow!
And the row
Starts
                    to
                                        GO

Dorothy W. Baruch

The Wheels of the Bus

The wheels of the bus go round and round,
Round and round, round and round,
The wheels of the bus go round and round,
All on a busy morning.

The people on the bus go up and down,
Up and down, up and down,
The people on the bus go up and down,
All on a busy morning.

The baby on the bus goes, "Wah, wah, wah;
Wah, wah, wah; wah, wah, wah;"
The baby on the bus goes, "Wah, wah, wah,"
All on a busy morning.

The horn on the bus says, "Toot, toot, toot;
Toot, toot, toot; toot, toot, toot;"
The horn on the bus says, "Toot, toot, toot,"
All on a busy morning.

The windshield wipers go, "Swish, swish, swish;
Swish, swish, swish; swish, swish, swish;"
The windshield wipers go, "Swish, swish, swish,"
All on a busy morning.

A Garage for Gabriel

by Catherine Woolley

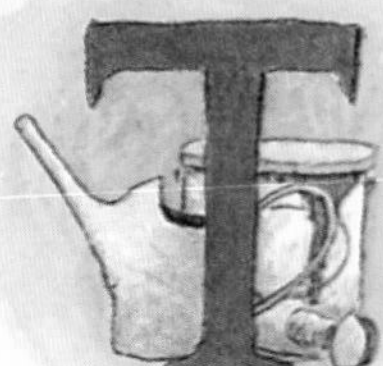

There was once a little car whose name was Gabriel.

Now poor Gabriel had no garage. He lived outdoors in a lot where they sold used cars. He wore a sign that said, "FOR SALE—CHEAP."

There were dents in his fenders. His paint was rusty. His doors sagged.

Every day Gabriel watched the shiny new cars roll by. But they never even looked at Gabriel.

"Oh," thought Gabriel, "how I should like to go whizzing right along. How I wish I were new and shiny!"

"But, specially," he thought sadly, "how I, *how* I wish I could have a garage!"

Well, one day two ladies came along.

They said to the man who sold cars, "Have you a small car?"

He pointed to Gabriel.

"We'll try it," they said. In they climbed.

"Now!" whispered Gabriel in great excitement. "I'll show them I can whiz right along. Then the ladies will buy me and give me a garage."

Whiz, whiz, whiz, went Gabriel around the block.

He was feeling mighty happy.

Round and round and round the block. *Whiz, whiz, whiz!*

"That will show them," he thought.

But the ladies cried, "Mercy, we don't want this car. It won't slow down at all."

Gabriel felt very sad.

Next day a college boy came.

"Here's a fine car," said the man.

"I'll try it," said the college boy.

"Oh, ho!" thought Gabriel. "This time I'll go very slowly, if that's what they want. Then the college boy will buy me and give me a garage."

So he went v-e-r-y, v–e–r–y, v—e—r—y,
s——l——o——w——l——y.

But the college boy said, "That car's too slow!"

And off he marched.

Gabriel felt very sad.

But the next day a young lady came.

This time Gabriel was determined to do the right thing.

"I won't go too fast and I won't go too slow," he said. "But I'll show her I've got pep in my engine. Then she'll buy me and give me a garage."

The young lady started the engine.

"BANG!" shouted Gabriel. "BANG, BING, BANG, POP, POP!"

"My goodness!" cried the young lady. "This car's much too noisy!"

And off she hurried.

"Oh, dear!" cried poor Gabriel. "Won't *anyone* ever buy me and give me a garage? I'll never be so noisy again!"

So the next day when a man came and pressed the starter, Gabriel didn't make any noise. Not *any* noise.

"This car won't even start," said the man. He turned on his heel and left.

Well, Gabriel felt just awful. Now he was sure that he never would have a garage.

And then Jimmy and Jimmy's daddy came along.

"Have you a car for $50?" asked Jimmy's daddy.

The man was so *mad* at Gabriel, he said, "Yes—*there's* a car for $50."

"Sold!" cried Jimmy's daddy.

They climbed right in.

Gabriel was so surprised that he never had time to show off. He just acted natural.

They drove up the street and stopped in front of a little yellow house.

Then Jimmy's daddy greased Gabriel's engine till it purred like a pussycat.

"I sound real quiet!" thought Gabriel.

Then Jimmy's daddy hammered out the dents in the fenders, and oiled the hinges and fixed the sagging doors.

"I feel real good!" whispered Gabriel.

And last of all, Jimmy's daddy gave Gabriel a coat of shiny red paint.

"I look FINE!" shouted Gabriel.

Then Jimmy and his daddy and mommy and Pooch, their cat, all went for a ride.

Every time they whizzed by another car, Gabriel bowed and smiled and the other cars bowed and smiled, too.

And when they came home, they whizzed right up the driveway into a little, yellow garage!

DOWN BY THE STATION

Down by the station, early in the morning,
See the little puffer bellies all in a row.
See the engine driver pull the little handle,
Puff, puff, choo, choo, and off they go.

First little train carries cars across the river,

Second little train brings sugar to the town.

Third little train carries books for the schoolhouse,

Fourth little train has costumes for a clown.

Fifth little train takes wheat to the baker,

Sixth little train brings fish from the bay.

Seventh little train carries pigs and cows and horses,

Eighth little train brings mail every day.

Ninth little train carries coal from the coal mines,
Tenth little train takes families to the shore.
Ten little puffer trains, a-chugging and a-chooing,
Puffing down the track and home once more!

An Adaptation of the Traditional Song

I PACKED MY VAN

A Silly Game to Play

I packed my van from A to Z.
What went in it? Look and see!

An Apple-eating Aardvark

An Apple-eating Aardvark and
A Blue Box of Black Binoculars

An Apple-eating Aardvark
A Blue Box of Black Binoculars and
A Case of Cheddar Cheese and a Carton of Coconut Cookies

An Apple-eating Aardvark
A Blue Box of Black Binoculars
A Case of Cheddar Cheese and a Carton of Coconut Cookies and
Dishes with Daffodils and Daisies

An Apple-eating Aardvark
A Blue Box of Black Binoculars
A Case of Cheddar Cheese and a Carton of Coconut Cookies
Dishes with Daffodils and Daisies and
Eight Enamel Eggs

An Apple-eating Aardvark
A Blue Box of Black Binoculars
A Case of Cheddar Cheese and a Carton of Coconut Cookies
Dishes with Daffodils and Daisies
Eight Enamel Eggs and
Four Fancy Frames

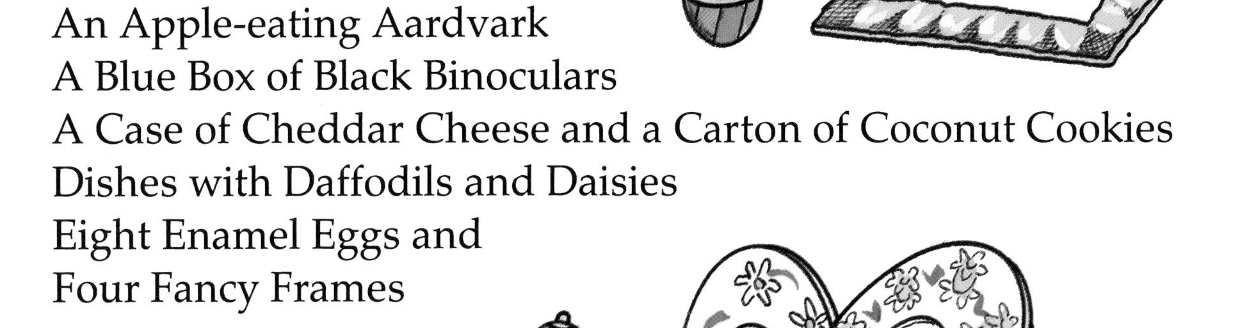

What else can you pack in your van? Turn the page and see!

An Apple-eating Aardvark
A Blue Box of Binoculars
A Case of Cheddar Cheese and a Carton of Coconut Cookies
Dishes with Daffodils and Daisies
Eight Enamel Eggs
Four Fancy Frames
. . . Green Gloves and Gold Goblets
. . . A Huge Harp
. . . Ice-cold Ice Cream
. . . A Jug of Juice
. . . A Keg of Ketchup
. . . Lace and Lavender Linen
. . . A Marble Mandolin and a Monkey Marionette
. . . Nine New Neckties
. . . Orange Overalls and Oily Olives
. . . Paisley Pajamas, a Pail of Purple Paint, and a Plaid Parachute
. . . A Quart of Quarters
. . . A Red Refrigerator
. . . Six Spicy Salami Sandwiches and Seven Speckled Snails
. . . Two Tall Telescopes and Ten Turquoise Tulips
. . . An Umbrella with Ukuleles
. . . A Velvet Vest and a Vat of Volleyballs
. . . A White Wooden Wheelbarrow
. . . A Xylophone
. . . Yellow Yarn
. . . And a Zither-playing Zebra!

You can play this game, too. Start with the letter **A** *and think of something to pack that starts with* **A**. *Then think of something that starts with the letter* **B**. *Keep going until you get to the letter* **Z**.

A Modern Dragon

A train is a dragon that roars through the dark.
He wriggles his tail as he sends up a spark.
He pierces the night with his one yellow eye,
And all the earth trembles when he rushes by.

Rowena Bennett

Trains

Over the mountains,
Over the plains,
Over the rivers,
Here come the trains.

Carrying passengers,
Carrying mail,
Bringing their precious loads
In without fail.

Thousands of freight cars
All rushing on
Through day and darkness
Through dusk and dawn.

Over the mountains,
Over the plains,
Over the rivers,
Here come the trains.

James S. Tippett

FLYING

Mom is taking me on my first trip in an airplane. We're going to visit Aunt June and Uncle Rusty! I can see the plane from the airport window. It's huge! I follow Mom to a door, where a smiling man dressed in a blue suit takes our tickets. We have to walk through a long tunnel to get into the plane.

The inside of the plane looks a lot different from the outside. We squeeze through a narrow aisle to get to our seats. Many people are putting small suitcases in compartments over their seats. I get to sit by the window! "Time to fasten our seat belts," Mom tells me.

I look out the window and see that we are moving. "We are driving to the runway," Mom says. "I never knew planes had wheels," I tell her. At the runway, the plane's engines begin to roar. The whole plane shakes! Down the runway we go. Zoom! We're going so fast that trees look like a blur of color. Then everything gets quiet. And we're up in the air. We're flying! I hear, *Bump! Bump!* My mom tells me that the wheels have gone inside the bottom of the plane.

Outside my window, everything looks tiny. Buildings look like toys, and cars look like ants. "That's because we're so high up," Mom says. Then all I see are clouds, soft and fluffy like cotton candy! "It doesn't feel like we're moving," I say. Mom says, "We're going faster than you've ever gone before."

A flight attendant takes me to meet the plane's pilots. They sit in the front part of the plane, which is called the cockpit. In the cockpit are panels with hundreds of dials, buttons, and levers. "All of these help us fly the jet," one of the pilots tells me.

Soon I go back to my seat. "Get ready for landing," says a voice over the loudspeaker. I fasten my seat belt. *Bump! Bump!* There go the wheels. The plane glides onto the runway and goes fast, then slower, and then it stops. The trip is over.

I can't wait to fly again!

AN AIRPLANE

Pretend you are an airplane. Where will you go? You can play this little hand game and pretend to fly to Mexico. Just follow the instructions as you say the verse. Zoom! Zoom!

If I had an airplane,
Zoom, zoom, zoom,
I would fly to Mexico,
Wave my hand and off I'd go.
If I had an airplane,
Zoom, zoom, zoom.

If I had an airplane,
Zoom, zoom, zoom...
(Extend right hand in front of body, palm opened flat, facing down.)

I would fly to Mexico...
(Fly hand through air like an airplane.)

Wave my hand and off I'd go.
(Wave to people.)

If I had an airplane . . .
(Repeat first instruction, using left hand.)

Zoom, zoom, zoom.
(Fly hand through air like an airplane.)

I Saw a Ship A'Sailing

by Teddy Gautier

"Call me captain," said the duck to his wife.

"You're no captain 'round here!" she quacked. "Get out of the nest!"

"Call me captain," said the duck to the farmer.

"You're no captain 'round here, squirt!" the farmer said. "Get out of the way!"

"Call me captain," said the duck to the geese.

"Captain, indeed!" they hissed. "Vamoose! Out of the pond!"

The duck waddled sadly about the fields and pasture, until finally he stepped into the barn for a little peace and quiet. But there he came upon twenty-four white mice, playing a game of cards. They wore red scarves around their necks and gladly shouted, "Gin!"

"Aye, they're so little," said the duck to himself, "that they'll do just what I say. I'll tell them I'm a captain, and make them do things my way."

But when the duck quacked loudly, the mice squealed and ran.

"Don't be afraid, mates!" he roared through the din. "I'm just an old sea captain, calling you aboard!"

"Where?" asked the mice. "Where do we sail?"

"Timbuktu!" said the duck. "Pack your worldly goods and come!"

Well, no mouse can refuse a bidding to a cruise. So they gathered all their treasures – apples, silk, and gold – and followed Captain Duck to a rowboat near a cove.

"Paddle, all of you!" Captain Duck bellowed. "Twelve mice to an oar!"

"What? That's no fun! Farewell, you unlucky duck!" shouted the mice in their high squeaky voices.

"Stop!" shouted the duck, about to lose his temper. Then he waved his wings in front of the mice and tried to hypnotize them. "You are in my power," he said slowly. "You will all row this boat."

All the mice began to laugh. Soon they were laughing so hard they couldn't move. They just sat in the boat and laughed and laughed. The duck grew very discouraged.

Well, needless to say, the voyage did not proceed; and the boat did not leave the cove. The mice laughed until the moon rose in the sky. Then they all went home to bed.

"It seems," said the duck to himself, waddling alone by the shore, "that being the one in charge has limited reward. I wish I hadn't been the captain and had simply asked them if I could play cards. I'd like to wear a red scarf and act like just another sailor."

When the duck returned to his wife, he knew she would not believe his tale. So he sat up all night and wrote a poem instead.

"In a poem," he realized, "your fondest dreams actually can come true."

So here is the famous poem of the now-famous Captain Duck:

I saw a ship a'sailing,
A'sailing on the sea;
And, oh, it was all laden
With pretty things for thee!
There were comfits in the cabin,
And apples in the hold;
The sails were made of silk,
And the masts were made of gold.
The four-and-twenty sailors
That stood between the decks,
Were four-and-twenty white mice
With chains about their necks.
The captain was a duck,
With a packet on his back;
And when the ship began to move,
The captain said,
''Quack! Quack!''

THE OCEAN LINER

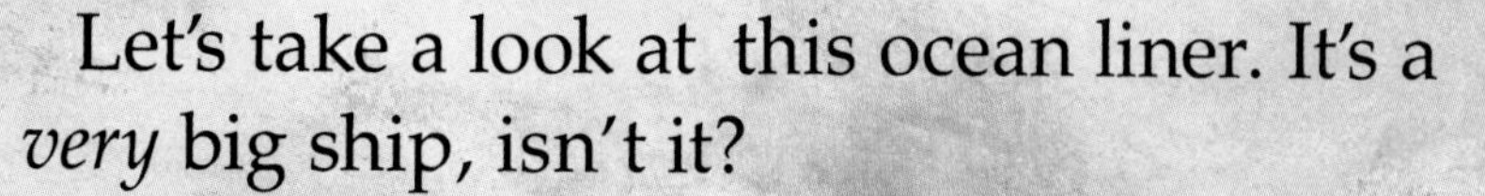

Let's take a look at this ocean liner. It's a *very* big ship, isn't it?

Ocean liners are like hotels. But they travel all over the world!

The captain is in charge of the ship. He has a big group of workers, called a crew, to help him.

Find the highest point on this ship. It's called the mast. The mast is used for many things. It holds lights so that helicopters, planes, and other ships can see the ocean liner at night. The mast also holds flags. Just below the mast is the bridge, which is where the captain runs the ship.

Do you see the rudder? The rudder moves back and forth when the captain turns the wheel. It changes the direction the ship is going in. Now look at the propeller. The spinning of the propeller makes the ship move.

Sometimes ocean liners stop at towns, or "ports," along the way. When an ocean liner comes into a port, the captain shuts down the engine and lowers the anchor. The anchor then hooks into the sand on the ocean floor. This makes the ship stay in place. Can you find the anchor in the picture?

On an ocean liner, you have lots to do. You can play basketball or even go swimming in a pool. What other activity rooms can you find?

If you were hungry, you would eat in the dining room. And at bedtime, you would go to your bedroom. Bedrooms on ocean liners are called cabins. Find the cabins in the pictures. Which one would you like to sleep in?

Wouldn't it be fun to travel on an ocean liner?

When We Work

Trucks

Big trucks for steel beams,
Big trucks for coal,
Rumbling down the broad streets,
Heavily they roll.

Little trucks for groceries,
Little trucks for bread,
Turning into every street,
Rushing on ahead.

Big trucks, little trucks,
In never ending lines,
Rumble on and rush ahead
While I read their signs.

James S. Tippett

WORK VEHICLES

Look at all those vehicles at work! Can you find the yellow school bus? The kids on the bus are looking for different kinds of vehicles. You can help the kids find them.

Search the city streets for the red fire truck with its big ladders. Now find the construction site. The workers are using a big crane to lift heavy loads to the top of a building. Do you see it? Can you find the tugboat in the harbor? It's guiding a big ocean liner to a dock.

Where are the two helicopters? Do you see the plane with six round windows? There's an ice-cream truck on the busy city streets. It has a big cone on its roof. Can you find it?

There are so many different kinds of work vehicles!

F is the Fighting Firetruck

F is the fighting Firetruck
That's painted a flaming red.
When the signals blast
It follows fast
When the chief flies on ahead.
And buses pull to the curbing
At the siren's furious cry,
For early or late
They have to wait
When the Firetruck flashes by.

Phyllis McGinley

A Special Ride for the Fire Dog

by Morgan Matthews

rf! Arf!" barked Sparky as he followed Fire Chief Smith over to a shiny, red car. Today was a special day for the young dalmatian. Sparky was bred to be a fire dog. And today Sparky was moving from the kennel, where he was raised, to a real firehouse.

"Let's go, Sparky," Chief Smith said. He opened the car door. Sparky hopped onto the seat and sat there proudly. He had waited for this special trip ever since he was a wee pup. Would Chief Smith sound the siren? Would he make the red lights spin and flash? Would people point and wave as they went by?

"Here we go," the chief said as he started the car. Varoom! Away they drove. But during the ride, the chief did not sound the siren or flash the lights. People didn't even notice as the car went by. Poor Sparky felt a bit sad.

"Why do you look unhappy?" Chief Smith said to Sparky. "Did you want to hear the sirens blare and see the red lights flash?"

"ARF!" barked Sparky excitedly.

"I'm sorry," said the Chief. "It's against the rules to flash the lights and sound the siren except for emergencies like going to a fire."

Sparky was disappointed, but he understood. A rule must be followed. He would have to wait for his special ride.

Before long, the red car arrived at Fire Station Number 28. Chief Smith parked his car. He and Sparky climbed out and went into the firehouse. Inside the firehouse were four red fire trucks. One of the trucks was a "pumper" with hoses running along the sides and folded up on the back, waiting to be connected to a fire hydrant. Another was a very big "hook-and-ladder" truck with long, long ladders on the top and sides. "I would like to ride on that big, red truck," thought Sparky.

"Come and meet Sparky, everyone," Chief Smith called. The fire fighters gathered around, and one by one they petted Sparky and

scratched behind his ears. "He is going to be a very good fire dog," Chief Smith said.

"ARF!" barked Sparky. He wanted to be a good fire dog. But most of all, he wanted to ride on that big, red fire truck.

BONG! BONG! BONG! An alarm suddenly sounded. "It's a fire!" Chief Smith shouted to the fire fighters. "Let's go!" Everyone quickly dressed in fireproof helmets, heavy rubber coats with bright, yellow stripes, and sturdy, waterproof boots. Then they strapped on big air tanks with masks so they could breathe at the smoky fire.

The big doors of the firehouse flipped open. The fire fighters jumped onto the trucks. Sparky barked and leaped onto the bright red hook and ladder.

"No, no, Sparky," said Chief Smith. "Get down. It is against the rules to take a dog to a fire. You will have to stay here."

Poor Sparky! He wanted to go, but he had to stay at the firehouse. A good fire dog always follows the rules. Off the truck he jumped.

AWHIRRR! screeched the sirens. BLINK! BLINK! Red lights began to flash. Varoom! Varoom! Out of the firehouse rumbled the trucks. Sparky sadly watched them speed away. "Will I ever get that special ride?" he wondered.

Time after time the fire trucks went out to fight fires. Every time the trucks went out, Sparky stayed behind at the firehouse. Sparky was happy to be a fire dog. He liked Chief Smith and the other fire fighters. But, more than anything, Sparky wanted to go for a special ride on the fire truck.

One day all the people of Fire Station Number 28 got up early. They shined and polished the fire trucks. They dressed in their best uniforms. When all the work was done, the big firehouse doors were opened. The fire fighters got on the fire trucks and started the motors. Varoom! Varoom! "Where are they going?" thought Sparky. "I didn't hear the alarm."

Chief Smith walked up. "Let's go, Sparky!" he said. Sparky couldn't believe his ears. He obediently followed Chief Smith over to the big, red fire truck. "Get on the truck, boy," Chief Smith said. "Today is a very important occasion. It is the day of the Fire Fighters' Parade. Our fire dog always rides in a special place of honor on our truck."

"ARF!" barked Sparky happily as he jumped up on the big, red fire truck. A good fire dog always follows the rules.

AWHIRRR! went the sirens. BLINK! BLINK! flashed the lights as the fire truck pulled out. Down the street they went. Everyone they passed pointed and waved at the proud fire dog sitting on the big, red fire truck.

Sparky the fire dog was getting his special ride at last!

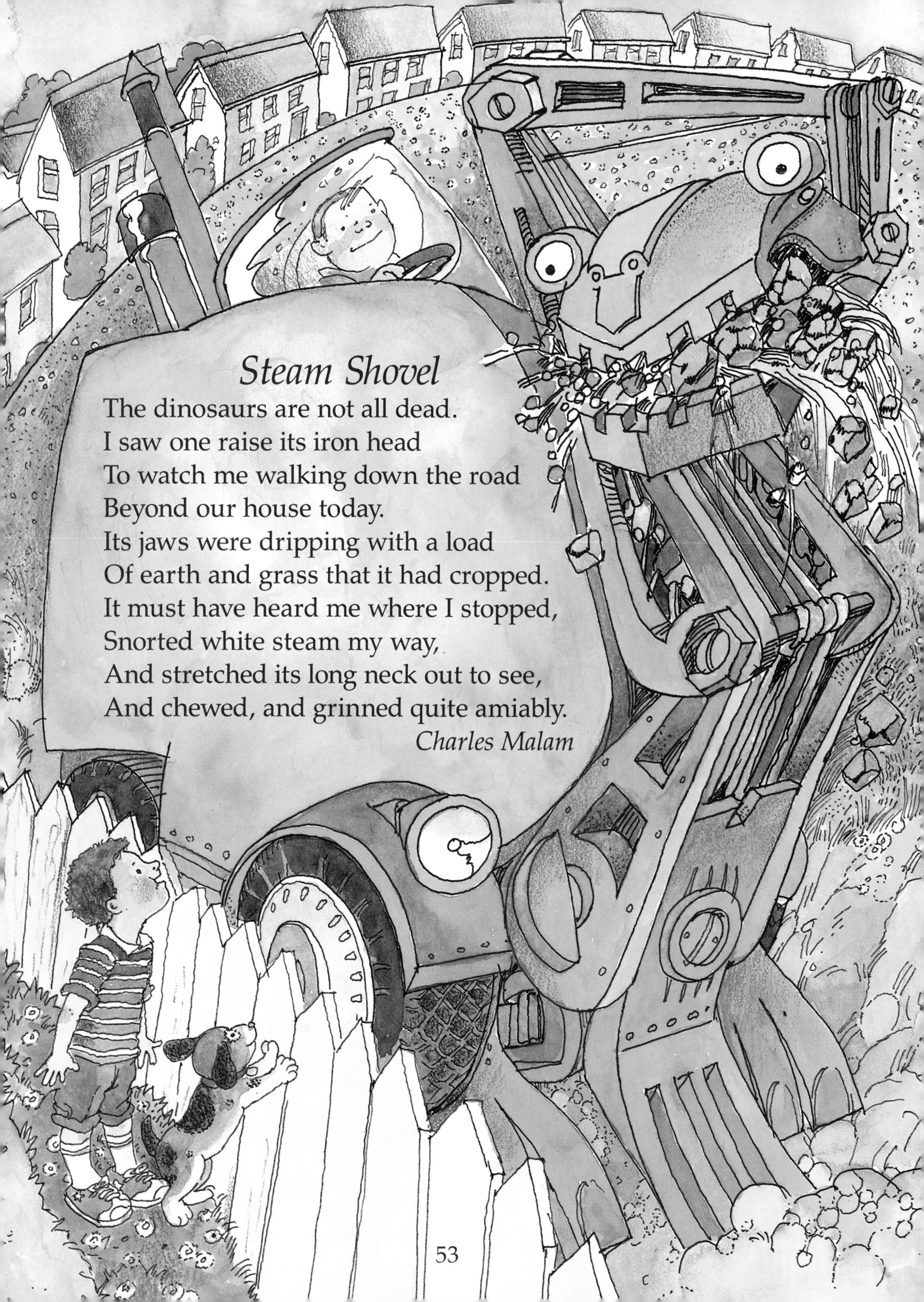

Steam Shovel

The dinosaurs are not all dead.
I saw one raise its iron head
To watch me walking down the road
Beyond our house today.
Its jaws were dripping with a load
Of earth and grass that it had cropped.
It must have heard me where I stopped,
Snorted white steam my way,
And stretched its long neck out to see,
And chewed, and grinned quite amiably.

Charles Malam

Rattle, Bump, and Roll

by Michael J. Pellowski

"Boring," groaned little Teddy Taylor as she walked to her school bus stop. "Boring! Boring! Boring! Every day, it's the same boring thing. Everyone waits by the big empty lot on Main Street. The old, gray school van drives up. We take a long, boring ride to school." Teddy sighed. "Why can't the ride be more fun?"

When Teddy neared her bus stop, she saw something new. A high, wooden fence surrounded the empty lot. All the kids at the bus stop were peeking into the lot through big round holes in the fence. Inside the fence, people were busy working. They were putting up a new building. As they worked, strange noises echoed out of big holes in the fence. Rattle! Rattle! Clankety-clank! Bumpity-bump! Crunch! Rumble-tumble! Toot!

"What curious sounds," thought the little girl. Standing on her toes, Teddy peeked through a hole in the fence. She saw people driving big, rumbling work machines.

Teddy smiled. What fun it would be to ride to school in one of those work machines. A ride like that would not be boring! How could anything that exciting be boring?

Mrs. Green, Teddy's teacher, would be so surprised if Teddy rode up in a huge crane. Clankety-clank! Teddy would not have to climb stairs to go to the second floor. The huge crane could lift her up as high as the roof.

Teddy grinned and thought some more. "I'd like to ride in the back of that bumpity-bump dump truck," she said to herself. "The truck could back up to the school's front door. Pop! The back would lift up. Wheee! Down I would slide into school!"

Rattle! Rattle! Rattle! rumbled the big, noisy power shovel as it went by. "Riding the power shovel would be exciting, too. All the other kids would point and laugh when they saw it coming," Teddy thought gleefully. She watched the power shovel bite into the earth and life up huge chunks of dirt. She giggled, thinking about recess. What a hole she could dig in the playground sandbox with that!

Crunch! The heavy steamroller was riding around, making the ground flat. It was big and noisy, just like the power shovel. Teddy thought about riding to school in it. "If I rode a steamroller to school, I would shout, 'Look out! Teddy is coming!' And everyone would scramble out of my way!"

Rumble-tumble! Rumble-tumble! Rumble-tumble! The cement mixer was busy mixing cement. "A ride to school in a cement mixer would be fun," said Teddy. "It looks like a dinosaur! It would never be as boring as riding in that old, gray school van."

BEEP! BEEP! BEEP! The honking noise was the sound of Teddy's ride to school. Teddy sighed and turned around. But something was strange. Where was her old, boring school van?

A brand new, shiny, yellow school bus was waiting at the corner in the van's place. BING! BING! It had bright red flashing lights on it.

"Come on, Teddy!" called the driver. "Hop in. It's time to go to school."

"Where is the van?" asked Teddy as she ran toward the bus.

"The old van is gone," said the driver. "From now on, we will ride to school in this brand new, shiny, yellow bus!"

"Wow!" said Teddy as she climbed on. "A ride in a big new bus can't be boring!"

The doors closed. They started off. Rattle! Bumpity! Rumble! Away they went. The bus couldn't dig like the power shovel. It didn't have a big arm like the crane. It couldn't flatten the ground like the steamroller. But it was big and yellow, just like some of the big work machines. And Teddy had such fun riding to school in it!

TAKE OFF WITH THE SPACE SHUTTLE

Would you like to take a trip to outer space?

There's a new kind of plane that can take you there in a jiffy. It's called the space shuttle. It can fly very, very fast.

How fast?

Say the words "one two" out loud.

In the time it takes you to say "one two," the shuttle can fly from here up to the clouds.

The shuttle has a lot of room inside because it carries big satellites into space. There's enough room for eight elephants!

On Earth, gravity keeps you on the ground. But there is no gravity in space. So astronauts float from one place to another inside the shuttle.

Outer space can be very cold. It can also be very hot. Sometimes the outside of the shuttle gets so hot that it turns bright red. But the shuttle has a special coat. This coat keeps the inside of the shuttle nice and comfortable no matter how cold or hot it is.

Right now, only astronauts can ride the shuttle. But by the time you're a grownup, everyone may be able to ride. So strap on your helmet! Fasten your seat belt! And get set to blast off into space!

MEET A MOON BUGGY

Look up at the sky. See the moon? It's very, very far away. Astronauts are the only people who have been to the moon. They've walked around on it. They've even driven around on it, in moon buggies!

Moon buggies are small, funny-looking cars. Each one has room for two astronauts. They also have room for the astronauts' tools. There are rakes for scraping away moon dust. There are drills for making holes in the moon. And there are bags for gathering moon rocks. The moon buggy even has a movie camera on it. The astronauts take pictures of everything they see to show people what the moon looks like.

The astronauts drove for many miles in their moon buggies. They visited the moon's mountains and valleys. The moon buggies made tracks in the dirt on the moon's surface. On Earth, the wind would blow these tracks away. Or the rain would wash them away. But on the moon, there is no wind and there is no rain. The tracks will just stay there, forever.

A TRUCK FULL OF RIDDLES

Here's a special delivery just for you—silly riddles about trucks and other work vehicles. See if you can guess the answers.

When is a police car not a police car?
When it turns into a driveway!

What kind of truck has four wheels and flies?
A garbage truck!

What did one tractor say to the other tractor?
"Hay!"

What did the ocean say to the helicopter overhead?
Nothing—it just waved!

When is a machine like a lazy cow?
When it's a bulldozer!

Why couldn't the bug walk across the inside of the cement mixer?
It was too hard!

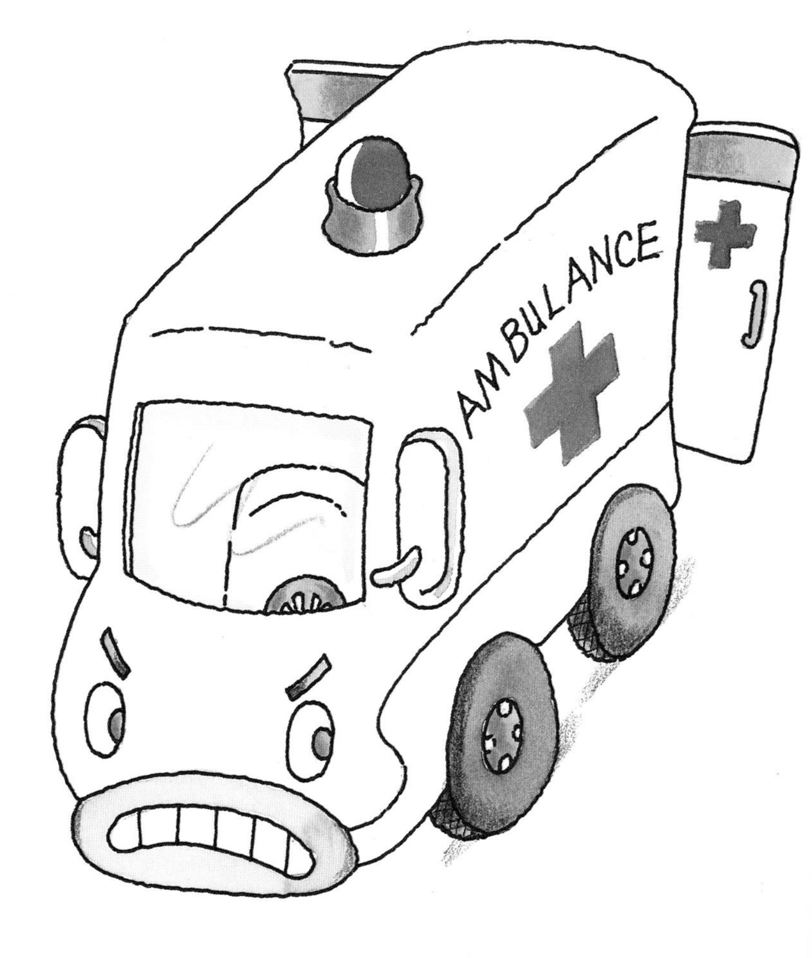

Why did the ambulance get angry whenever it was empty?
It was out of patients!

What seven letters did the snowplow say to the snowy road?
O.I.C.U.R.I.C.!

Why did the fire fighters on the fire truck all wear red suspenders?
To keep their pants up!

Little People™ Big Book About THINGS WE RIDE

PRODUCED BY PARACHUTE PRESS, INC.

Editorial Director: Joan Waricha
Editors: Christopher Medina, Jane Stine
Writers: Kathy Dubowski, Lisa Eisenberg, Teddy Gautier, Joan Israel, Michael J. Pellowski, Joan Powers, Jean Waricha, Eric Weiner
Designer: Deborah Michel
Illustrators: Yvette Banek, Carolyn Bracken, Molly Delaney, Steve Petruccio, Roz Shaunzer, John Speirs

ACKNOWLEDGMENTS

Every effort has been made to trace the ownership of all copyrighted material and to secure the necessary permissions to reprint these selections. If any question arises as to the use of any material, the editor and the publisher, while expressing regret for any inadvertent error, will make the necessary correction in future printings.

Grateful acknowledgment is made to the following for permission to reprint the copyrighted material listed below: Kenneth C. Bennett for "A Modern Dragon" by Rowena Bennett. Curtis Brown Ltd. for "F is the Fighting Firetruck" by Phyllis McGinley. Copyright © 1948, 1976 by Phyllis McGinley. E.P. Dutton, a division of Penguin Books USA Inc. for "There Are So Many Ways of Going Places" by Leslie Thompson. Copyright © 1937 by E.P. Dutton, renewed 1965 by Lucy Sprague Mitchell. Harper & Row for "Trains" and "Trucks" from CRICKETY CRICKET: THE BEST LOVED POEMS OF JAMES S. TIPPETT. Copyright © 1929 by Harper & Row, renewed 1957, 1959 by James S. Tippett. Henry Holt & Co. for "Steam Shovel" from UPPER PASTURE: POEMS by Charles Malam. Copyright © 1930, 1958 by Charles Malam. Bertha Klausner International Literary Agency for "Stop-Go" by Dorothy Baruch. Lois Lenski Covey Foundation for "Riding On My Bike" by Lois Lenski. Copyright © 1965 by Lois Lenski. Robert Luce Inc. for "An Airplane" from LET'S DO FINGERPLAYS by Marion Grayson. Copyright © 1962 by Marion Grayson. Catherine Woolley for "A Garage for Gabriel." Copyright © 1947 by Catherine Woolley, renewed 1952 by Wonder Books.

Library of Congress Cataloging-in-Publication Data

Little people big book about things we ride.
p. cm.
Summary: A collection of original stories, essays, poems, questions and answers, activities, and games about various forms of transportation.
ISBN 0-8094-7462-X.—ISBN 0-8094-7463-8 (lib. bdg.)
1. Transportation—Literary collections. [1. Transportation—Literary collections.] I. Time-Life for Children (Firm)
PZ5.L7259 1989
808.8'0355—dc20

89-37470
CIP
AC

TIME-LIFE BOOKS
ALEXANDRIA, VIRGINIA

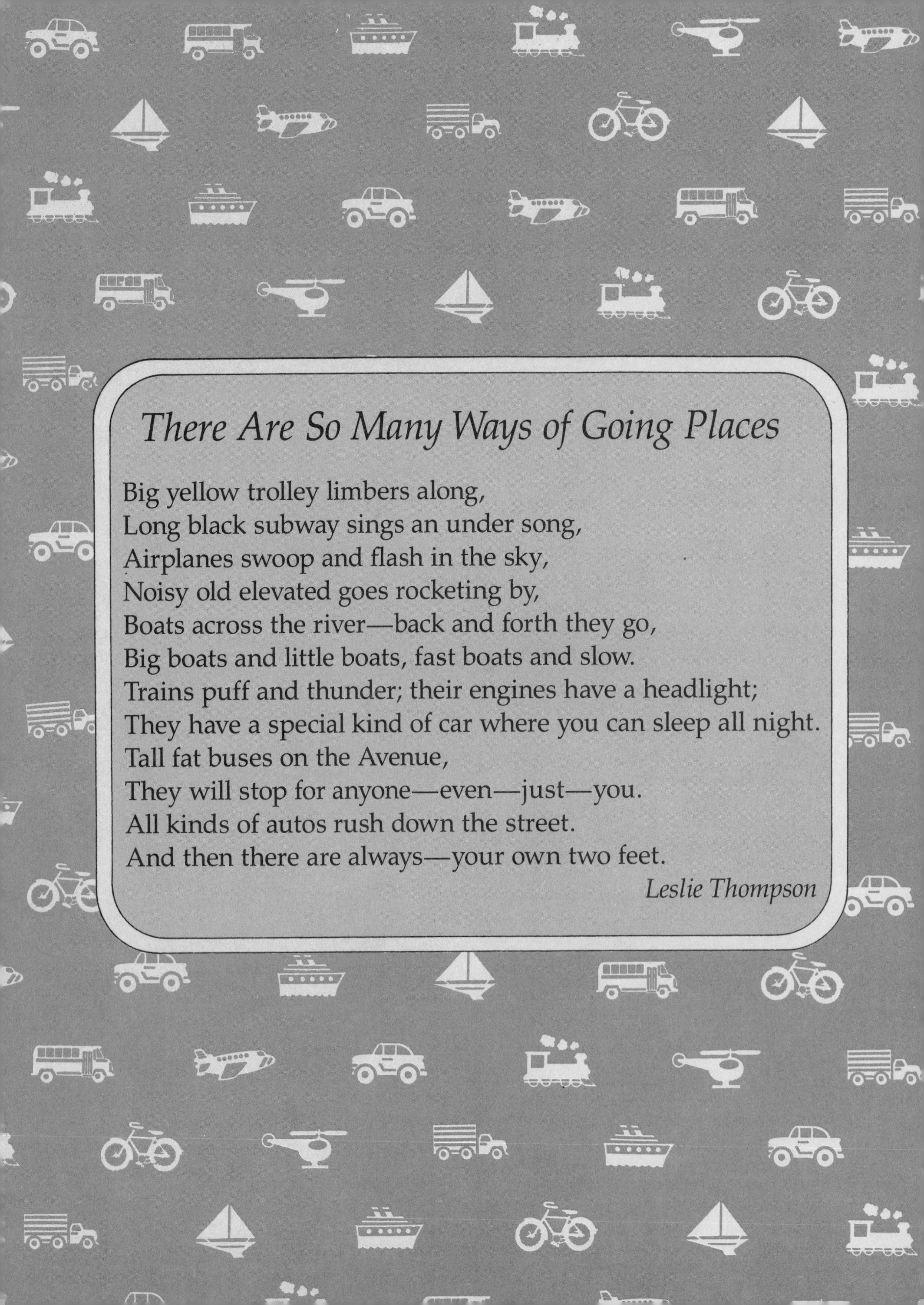

There Are So Many Ways of Going Places

Big yellow trolley limbers along,
Long black subway sings an under song,
Airplanes swoop and flash in the sky,
Noisy old elevated goes rocketing by,
Boats across the river—back and forth they go,
Big boats and little boats, fast boats and slow.
Trains puff and thunder; their engines have a headlight;
They have a special kind of car where you can sleep all night.
Tall fat buses on the Avenue,
They will stop for anyone—even—just—you.
All kinds of autos rush down the street.
And then there are always—your own two feet.

Leslie Thompson